D0866426

Excerpts from the King's Mirror

The Vikings'
Guide to Good
Business

Excerpts from the King's Mirror

THE
VIKINGS'
GUIDE
TO GOOD
BUSINESS

Translated from the original 13th-century text
by Bernard Scudder

English translation © Bernard Scudder 1997

Edited by Björn Jonasson
Cover design and layout: Helgi Hilmarsson and Björn Jonasson

© GUDRUN 1997
Reykjavík – Göteborg – Oslo – København

ISBN 9979-856-22-X (Hard cover)

Berkeley 6-24p – Goudy 14p – Charlemagne

Printed in Iceland
by Oddi Ltd. Printing Press

Index

Preface

This book contains excerpts from an old Nordic text called the King's Mirror, which was a compilation of advice and wisdom for various classes of society, including merchants, men at the royal court and scholars. Written about 1240, the King's Mirror describes or reflects the society of its day and is largely a prescription for ethical behaviour.

During the four or five hundred years between the beginning of the Viking Age and the writing of this manuscript, the peoples of the northern countries had extensive experience in trading. The huge expansion that began as mere armed raids gradually evolved into participation in the European power struggle, in which the Nordic nations played a key role for some time. But the Viking voyages to no less an extent paved the way for extensive, organized trade.

By the time the King's Mirror was written, the Viking Age proper was over and a new era had begun, but the wisdom and experience that the Vikings had acquired lived on. Sailings to distant countries were typified the Viking Age and the Vikings developed navigational skills unparalleled in their day. Knowledge of sailing routes and features of local and national life grew at the same time. On basis of all this, the ascendancy of trading in the Baltic would later be built established.

This is the ancient wisdom presented in The Vikings' Guide to Good Business. The entire text is taken from orginal sources and only the chapter headings have been added. It is based on the editions published by Magnús Már Lárusson (Reykjavík 55). Illustrations are taken from Historia de Gentibus Septentrionalibus (Rome 1555) by Olaus Magnus.

Who are merchants?

The finest men often enter this class. But much depends on whether you resemble those who are true merchants, or others who call themselves merchants but are actually swindlers or cheats and trade falsely.

In unfamiliar countries

A merchant has to place himself in many perils. Sometimes at sea, sometimes in heathen lands, and almost always among unfamiliar peoples. He needs to seek out ways to be welcome wherever he goes.

Make yourself polite and easy-going

erchants need to show great boldness and strength at sea. But if you are in a town, or wherever you are, make yourself polite and easy-going. That will make you popular with all good men.

The merchant's morning tasks

ake a habit of waking up early and going straight to a church, wherever you think it best to hear prayers. Then listen to all the prayers and the mass straight after matins, and pray, using the psalms and the prayers that you know.

Watch the best men

nd when the prayers are over, go out and see to your business. But if you are unfamiliar with business in that town, observe carefully how the men who are considered the greatest and best merchants go about their business.

Take care about
the goods you buy

You should also take care that all the goods you buy are entirely sound and flawless, and inspect them before you finally buy them. And in all the purchases you make, always have some trustworthy men around as witnesses to the purchase.

Keep your table well

You shall keep your table well with white cloths, clean food and good drink. Become known for your table, if you have the chance.

Keep alert

fter dining, go
out for a
while, enjoy
yourself and see what
other good merchants
are doing or whether
any goods have arrived
which you need to buy.

Be cautious and honourable

hen you go
to your
room,
inspect your goods so that
they do not later suffer
flaws which will be attri-
buted to you. But if your
goods become flawed and
you sell them, never con-
ceal this from the buyer.
Show him the flaws and
then strike your bargain as
you can. Then you will not
be called a fraud.

Show moderation

Put a good price on all your goods, close to what you see can be obtained for them without being excessive. Then you will not be called a cheat.

Learning
from books

Whenever
you are
free to do
so, study – above all
books of law. The fact is
that no men are wiser
than those who acquire
their wisdom from books.
Learned men have the
most scope for showing
their knowledge.

Familiarize yourself with the law

amiliarize yourself with all books of law, and for as long as you are a merchant familiarize yourself with the Birka code. If you are familiar with the law, you will not be the victim of injustice when dealing with your equals, and you will know how to answer all matters in a lawful manner.

Adopt good customs

o man will be fully wise unless he has a firm grasp and command of local customs. And if you want to perfect your knowledge, master all languages, but above all Latin and French, for those languages can be used in most places. But do not forget your own language either.

Be active

ake a habit of being as active as you can, but not so much as to damage your health.

Be cheerful and light-hearted

Rarely be gloomy, because a gloomy disposition is always morbid. Instead, be cheerful and light-hearted, keep a balanced mind and never show extremes of temperament.

Choose good company

Be wary of reproaching others and teach good things to everyone who is willing to learn from you. Always be open to the company of the best men.

Guard your tongue

Guard your tongue carefully and know that this is a noble approach. For your tongue may do you honour or your tongue may condemn you. Even when you are angry, say little, and speak nothing rashly. For if a man is not careful, he may speak in anger one little word that he would later be willing to pay gold never to have said.

Keep your tongue from evil words

I do not know of any revenge which belittles a man more, though this is commonly done, than arguing with someone else, even when he is engaged in a dispute with his equals. You should also know that a man has no nobler or stronger power than to restrain his tongue firmly from swearing or evil words, jibes or other harsh language.

Do not let your child grow up in ignorance

If you have children, do not let your child grow up without learning any skills, because a man has the greatest chance of developing wisdom or skills once he comes of age if he has been made aware of them while under someone's command.

Beware of heavy drinking and whores

gain there are things that you shall avoid like the devil himself — these are drinking, board games, whores, arguing and gambling. For on these foundations the greatest misfortunes are raised, and few men who do not avoid such things will live for long without reproach or sin.

Make yourself
sharp with figures

lso study
carefully
when daylight
falls, the movements of
the stars, the parts of
the day and the points
of the compass. Learn
also to recognize clearly
how much the sea calms
or swells, because this is
great knowledge and
essential to all who want
to travel and trade.
Make yourself sharp
with figures; this is
essential for merchants.

Make influential friends

If you happen to be where the agents of a king or other noblemen who rule that country are, make them your friends.

It is harder to seek pardon afterwards than to be cautious beforehand.

I f leaders demand to be paid duties on behalf of the ruler of the land, be prompt to render all such payments and contributions, to make sure that you do not hold on to small things only at the cost of large ones. Be careful that the king's belongings do not enter your purse, because you never know whether those who safeguard such interests will be greedy for money, and it is harder to seek pardon afterwards than to be cautious beforehand.

Never keep your goods in store for long

Never keep your goods in store for long if you can dispose of them at the right price, for it is the hallmark of a merchant always to buy and sell to others quickly.

Attract the best men

wn shares either in good ships, or in none at all. Make your ship attractive, then good people will join it and it will be well manned. Make your ship ready to sail at the beginning of summer and travel during the best part of the year, and always have reliable equipment on board. And never stay out on the high sea in autumn, if it is within your powers. Take good care of all these things – then there is hope that all will turn out well, with God's mercy.

If you wish to be called fully wise

You shall also certainly keep in mind that no day should ever pass in which you do not learn anything of use to you, if you wish to be called fully knowledgeable. And do not be like those men who regard it as an insult if others tell or teach them things which would be very useful to learn. Treat it as an honour to learn as much as to teach, if you wish to be called fully wise.

In a town

If you come to a town and intend to stay there, take a room where you hear that the landlord is most obliging and popular with both citizenry and the king's men. Always keep yourself well provided for in dress and food, if you can. Never have unpeaceful or unruly men at your table or in your party.

Be peaceful

Be peaceful your-
self, but never
so much that
you suffer damage or ac-
cusations of cowardice.
Even if necessity forces
you to be unpeaceful, do
not try to take quick re-
venge before you can see
that it will be achieved
and will be felt where it is
deserved. Do not be ag-
gressive if you see that
you cannot have your
way, and seek to establish
your honour, though it
may come later, unless
your rival makes you an
honourable offer.

If your money grows substantially

If your money grows substantially when you travel and trade, put it in partnerships in places where you do not go yourself, but show discretion in your choice of partner.

In company with God, the Virgin Mary and the saints

You shall always give God Almighty and the Virgin Mary a share of your wealth, as well as the saint you pray to most often. And guard carefully the money that saints share with you, and always send it securely to the places where it was originally promised.

Where shall money be put?

If you have much money when you go trading, divide it into three parts. Allocate one-third towards sharing with men who are always in good towns, are loyal to you and know how to trade. Then divide the other two parts between various places and trade voyages. There is least chance of everything being ruined if your money is in many places at once, and the most chance that it will remain intact in some places, even when crises often occur.

Put your money in
good land, because
such assets are most
often considered secure

But if you notice
that your money
begins to grow
substantially when you go
trading, take two parts of it
and put them in good land,
because such assets are
most often considered
secure, whether the merc-
hant himself or his family
shall enjoy them. Then you
may do as you please with
the third part, use it for
trading further or put it all
into land.

When your money has grown to the full

Though you wish to keep your money in trading for a long time, you should stop sailing or travelling among countries yourself when your money has grown to the full and you have studied the ways of men as you please. Remember carefully all the people you have seen, whether good or bad. Remember all evil customs so as to avoid them — but adopt all good customs for your own benefit and that of everyone who wishes to learn them from you.

Appendix

On the Birka code

The Birka code (Bjarkeyjarréttur) referred to on page 33 is the oldest civic law in Scandinavia. It is described as follows in the Nordic Cultural-Historical Encyclopaedia: "The original translation of the word Bjarkaeyjarréttur must have been 'the code applying to a place called Bjarkey.' Of all the places in Scandinavia which have borne this name, only one was influential enough to qualify, namely Bjarkey on Lake Mälaren in Sweden, where there was a farm called Birka. Most evidence suggests that the law passed for Nidaros [Trondheim] by King Ólafur Tryggvason of Norway in 997 was called the Birka code." Before the Norwegian Birka code was introduced, Birka was a well-known trading centre.

Located near what is now Stockholm, Birka was the first Viking trading centre along with Hedeby in Schleswig. Other well-known trading centres included Eketorp on Öland, Ribe on Jutland, Fotevik in southwest Sweden, Trelleborg on Zealand, Trelleborg in southwest Sweden and Dorestad on the River Rhine. These towns flourished during the Viking Age, the period when the Birka code came into being. The Birka code is primarily a legal code governing trade and trading centres.